2016 SQA Past Papers With Answers

National 5
COMPUTING SCIENCE

2014, 2015 & 2016 Exams

HODDER GIBSON
AN HACHETTE UK COMPANY

National 5 COMPUTING SCIENCE

This book contains the official SQA 2014, 2015 and 2016 Exams for National 5 Computing Science, with associated SQA-approved answers modified from the official marking instructions that accompany the paper.

In addition the book contains study skills advice. This advice has been specially commissioned by Hodder Gibson, and has been written by experienced senior teachers and examiners in line with the new National 5 syllabus and assessment outlines. This is not SQA material but has been devised to provide further guidance for National 5 examinations.

Hodder Gibson is grateful to the copyright holders, as credited on the final page of the Answer Section, for permission to use their material. Every effort has been made to trace the copyright holders and to obtain their permission for the use of copyright material. Hodder Gibson will be happy to receive information allowing us to rectify any error or omission in future editions.

Hachette UK's policy is to use papers that are natural, renewable and recyclable products and made from wood grown in sustainable forests. The logging and manufacturing processes are expected to conform to the environmental regulations of the country of origin.

Orders: please contact Bookpoint Ltd, 130 Park Drive, Milton Park, Abingdon, Oxon OX14 4SE. Telephone: (44) 01235 827720. Fax: (44) 01235 400454. Lines are open 9.00–5.00, Monday to Saturday, with a 24-hour message answering service. Visit our website at www.hoddereducation.co.uk. Hodder Gibson can be contacted direct on: Tel: 0141 333 4650; Fax: 0141 404 8188; email: hoddergibson@hodder.co.uk

This collection first published in 2016 by
Hodder Gibson, an imprint of Hodder Education,
An Hachette UK Company
211 St Vincent Street
Glasgow G2 5QY

Typeset by Aptara, Inc.

Printed in the UK

A catalogue record for this title is available from the British Library

ISBN: 978-1-4718-9105-2

3 2 1

2017 2016

Introduction

Study Skills – what you need to know to pass exams!

Pause for thought

Many students might skip quickly through a page like this. After all, we all know how to revise. Do you really though?

Think about this:

"IF YOU ALWAYS DO WHAT YOU ALWAYS DO, YOU WILL ALWAYS GET WHAT YOU HAVE ALWAYS GOT."

Do you like the grades you get? Do you want to do better? If you get full marks in your assessment, then that's great! Change nothing! This section is just to help you get that little bit better than you already are.

There are two main parts to the advice on offer here. The first part highlights fairly obvious things but which are also very important. The second part makes suggestions about revision that you might not have thought about but which WILL help you.

Part 1

DOH! It's so obvious but …

Start revising in good time

Don't leave it until the last minute – this will make you panic.

Make a revision timetable that sets out work time AND play time.

Sleep and eat!

Obvious really, and very helpful. Avoid arguments or stressful things too – even games that wind you up. You need to be fit, awake and focused!

Know your place!

Make sure you know exactly **WHEN and WHERE** your exams are.

Know your enemy!

Make sure you know what to expect in the exam.

How is the paper structured?

How much time is there for each question?

What types of question are involved?

Which topics seem to come up time and time again?

Which topics are your strongest and which are your weakest?

Are all topics compulsory or are there choices?

Learn by DOING!

There is no substitute for past papers and practice papers – they are simply essential! Tackling this collection of papers and answers is exactly the right thing to be doing as your exams approach.

Part 2

People learn in different ways. Some like low light, some bright. Some like early morning, some like evening / night. Some prefer warm, some prefer cold. But everyone uses their BRAIN and the brain works when it is active. Passive learning – sitting gazing at notes – is the most INEFFICIENT way to learn anything. Below you will find tips and ideas for making your revision more effective and maybe even more enjoyable. What follows gets your brain active, and active learning works!

Activity 1 – Stop and review

Step 1

When you have done no more than 5 minutes of revision reading STOP!

Step 2

Write a heading in your own words which sums up the topic you have been revising.

Step 3

Write a summary of what you have revised in no more than two sentences. Don't fool yourself by saying, "I know it, but I cannot put it into words". That just means you don't know it well enough. If you cannot write your summary, revise that section again, knowing that you must write a summary at the end of it. Many of you will have notebooks full of blue/black ink writing. Many of the pages will not be especially attractive or memorable so try to liven them up a bit with colour as you are reviewing and rewriting. **This is a great memory aid, and memory is the most important thing.**

Activity 2 – Use technology!

Why should everything be written down? Have you thought about "mental" maps, diagrams, cartoons and colour to help you learn? And rather than write down notes, why not record your revision material?

What about having a text message revision session with friends? Keep in touch with them to find out how and what they are revising and share ideas and questions.

Why not make a video diary where you tell the camera what you are doing, what you think you have learned and what you still have to do? No one has to see or hear it, but the process of having to organise your thoughts in a formal way to explain something is a very important learning practice.

Be sure to make use of electronic files. You could begin to summarise your class notes. Your typing might be slow, but it will get faster and the typed notes will be easier to read than the scribbles in your class notes. Try to add different fonts and colours to make your work stand out. You can easily Google relevant pictures, cartoons and diagrams which you can copy and paste to make your work more attractive and **MEMORABLE**.

Activity 3 – This is it. Do this and you will know lots!

Step 1

In this task you must be very honest with yourself! Find the SQA syllabus for your subject (www.sqa.org.uk). Look at how it is broken down into main topics called MANDATORY knowledge. That means stuff you MUST know.

Step 2

BEFORE you do ANY revision on this topic, write a list of everything that you already know about the subject. It might be quite a long list but you only need to write it once. It shows you all the information that is already in your long-term memory so you know what parts you do not need to revise!

Step 3

Pick a chapter or section from your book or revision notes. Choose a fairly large section or a whole chapter to get the most out of this activity.

With a buddy, use Skype, Facetime, Twitter or any other communication you have, to play the game "If this is the answer, what is the question?". For example, if you are revising Geography and the answer you provide is "meander", your buddy would have to make up a question like "What is the word that describes a feature of a river where it flows slowly and bends often from side to side?".

Make up 10 "answers" based on the content of the chapter or section you are using. Give this to your buddy to solve while you solve theirs.

Step 4

Construct a wordsearch of at least 10 × 10 squares. You can make it as big as you like but keep it realistic. Work together with a group of friends. Many apps allow you to make wordsearch puzzles online. The words and phrases can go in any direction and phrases can be split. Your puzzle must only contain facts linked to the topic you are revising. Your task is to find 10 bits of information to hide in your puzzle, but you must not repeat information that you used in Step 3. DO NOT show where the words are. Fill up empty squares with random letters. Remember to keep a note of where your answers are hidden but do not show your friends. When you have a complete puzzle, exchange it with a friend to solve each other's puzzle.

Step 5

Now make up 10 questions (not "answers" this time) based on the same chapter used in the previous two tasks. Again, you must find NEW information that you have not yet used. Now it's getting hard to find that new information! Again, give your questions to a friend to answer.

Step 6

As you have been doing the puzzles, your brain has been actively searching for new information. Now write a NEW LIST that contains only the new information you have discovered when doing the puzzles. Your new list is the one to look at repeatedly for short bursts over the next few days. Try to remember more and more of it without looking at it. After a few days, you should be able to add words from your second list to your first list as you increase the information in your long-term memory.

FINALLY! Be inspired...

Make a list of different revision ideas and beside each one write **THINGS I HAVE** tried, **THINGS I WILL** try and **THINGS I MIGHT** try. Don't be scared of trying something new.

And remember – "FAIL TO PREPARE AND PREPARE TO FAIL!"

National 5 Computing Science

The National 5 Computing Science exam is worth 90 marks. That is 60% of your overall mark. The remaining 40% of your overall mark (60 marks) comes from the supervised assignment which you will complete in class.

The exam

Approximately half of the marks in the question paper will be awarded for questions related to *Software Design and Development*, and half to *Information Systems Design and Development*.

Candidates will complete the question paper in 1 hour and 30 minutes.

Section 1 will have 20 marks and will consist of short answer questions assessing breadth of knowledge from across both Units. Most questions will have 1–2 marks.

Section 2 will have 70 marks and will consist of approximately 6–8 extended response questions, each with approximately 8–12 marks. Questions will be of a problem-solving nature rather than direct recall and will include extended descriptions and explanations.

Questions related to Software Design and Development will cover the following areas:

- computational constructs and concepts
- explaining code
- writing code
- data types and structures
- software development — design, testing, documentation
- low level operations and computer architecture.

Questions relating to coding will use the reference language for National 5 Computing Science question papers. Refer to this document on the SQA website for further information.

The only standard algorithm you need to know at National 5 is Input Validation.

If you have to write a solution to a problem in the examination, you can use a programming language you are familiar with. It is the constructs that are being assessed.

Questions related to Information Systems Design and Development will cover the following areas:

- database design, structures, links and operations
- website design, structures and links
- coding (including HTML and Javascript)
- media types, including file size calculations
- information system development — purpose, features, user interface, testing

- technical implementation (hardware, software, storage, networking/connectivity)
- security, legal and environmental issues.

General advice

Remember to read the questions carefully and answer what is being asked.

Trade names

It is never acceptable to use a company name, such as Microsoft Access or Serif Web-Plus etc. in an answer. Use the generic terms such as databases or web-design packages.

Conversion

If you are asked to convert a number into an 8-bit binary number make sure that your answer has 8 bits!

Technical terminology

It is important that the correct technical terminology is used e.g. USB flash drive – not USB pen, USB stick, pen drive or other commonly used expressions.

Units

Remember, there are 1024 bytes in a Kilobyte, not 1000. There are:

- 1024 Kilobytes in a Megabyte
- 1024 Megabytes in a Gigabyte
- 1024 Gigabytes in a Terabyte.

Data structure

The only data structure you need to know at National 5 is one-dimensional arrays.

Memory

Many candidates confuse RAM memory with backing storage. Remember, RAM memory is used to store programs and data temporarily while the program is being used. Backing storage is used to hold programs and data permanently until you are ready to use them. When you open an application it is taken from the backing storage (e.g. hard disc drive) and placed into the RAM memory.

Calculating storage requirements

When calculating the storage requirements for photographs, too many candidates forget that DPI must be squared. Remember to multiply the number of bits required to store the colour – NOT the number of colours!

For example, an image measures 3 inches by 4 inches and has a resolution of 600dpi in 8 colours

= 3 x 4 x 600 x 600 x 3 (3 bits can give 8 combinations of colours)

= 12960000 bits = 12960000/8 =1620000 bytes

= 1620000/1024 = 1582.03 Kb = 1882.03 / 1024

= 1.54 Mb

Computers and the Law

Candidates must give the correct full names of the appropriate laws and be able to give description, identification and implications for individuals and businesses for the "Data Protection Act", "Computer Misuse Act", "Health & Safety Regulations", "Communications Act" and "Copyright, Design and Patents Act".

Interfaces

Many candidates forget why an interface is required. Remember that an interface changes electrical voltages, changes analogue to digital, buffers data and deals with control signals. DO NOT confuse it with the Human Computer Interface.

Pre-defined functions

Remember that pre-defined functions (with parameters) are built-in sections of code that have been written and tested and are available for programmers to use. They include random, integer and round.

Good luck!

Remember that the rewards for passing National 5 Computing Science are well worth it! Your pass will help you get the future you want for yourself. In the exam, be confident in your own ability. If you're not sure how to answer a question, trust your instincts and just give it a go anyway. Keep calm and don't panic! GOOD LUCK!

NATIONAL 5

2014

N5

National
Qualifications
2014

Mark

X716/75/01

Computing Science

FRIDAY, 23 MAY

9:00 AM–10:30 AM

Fill in these boxes and read what is printed below.

Full name of centre

Town

Forename(s)

Surname

Number of seat

Date of birth
Day   Month   Year

| D | D | M | M | Y | Y |

Scottish candidate number

Total marks—90

SECTION 1—20 marks

Attempt ALL questions in this section.

SECTION 2—70 marks

Attempt ALL questions in this section.

Write your answers clearly in the spaces provided in this booklet. Additional space for answers is provided at the end of this booklet. If you use this space you must clearly identify the question number you are attempting.

Use **blue** or **black** ink.

Show all working.

Before leaving the examination room you must give this booklet to the Invigilator; if you do not, you may lose all the marks for this paper.

SQA

MARKS | DO NOT WRITE IN THIS MARGIN

SECTION 1 — 20 marks
Attempt ALL questions

1. A web page can use internal and external hyperlinks.

    Explain the difference between an internal hyperlink and external hyperlink.   **2**

    _____

    _____

    _____

2. Gillian is viewing a website on her laptop. Name the software on Gillian's laptop that enables her to do this.   **1**

    _____

3. Calculate the backing storage required for an 8 bit colour image 400 pixels by 600 pixels.

    Express your answer in Kilobytes.   **3**

4. Name the part of the processor that deals with comparisons.   **1**

    _____

MARKS

5. Convert the decimal value 47 into the equivalent 8-bit binary number.

1

6. State **one** problem associated with storing data in a flat file database.

1

_____

7. A bank employee has lost a laptop storing customers' personal details.

Identify **one** *security precaution* the bank should have in place to prevent unauthorised access to this information.

1

_____

_____

8. When ordering pizza online, users select their choice from the following drop down menu:

PIZZA ▽
Margherita
Hawaiian
Pepperoni

State **one** advantage of this type of user interface.

1

_____

_____

[Turn over

MARKS | DO NOT WRITE IN THIS MARGIN

9. Before going live with a new website, the developer makes sure it matches the original design. Describe **one** other type of testing that the developer should carry out.   1

_____

_____

10. Businesses and individuals are now making use of *cloud* services instead of local storage for storing their data.

    State **one** benefit of using cloud based storage instead of local storage.   1

_____

_____

11. Hussain is a technician for a new company and has been asked to prepare a presentation on networks. State **one** difference between peer-to-peer and client/server networks that he could include in his presentation.   2

Client/Server	Peer-to-Peer

MARKS

12.   This pseudocode allows a user to enter the level they wish to start playing a game.

> Line 1 RECEIVE level FROM (INTEGER) KEYBOARD
>
> Line 2 WHILE level < 1 OR level > 10 DO
>
> Line 3   SEND "error : please re-enter level" TO DISPLAY
>
> Line 4   RECEIVE level FROM (INTEGER) KEYBOARD
>
> Line 5 END WHILE

Explain what happens if a user enters 12.   2

13.   A programmer is developing a stock control program. If a user enters a stock code number from 1 to 900, it will display the number of items in stock.

Give **one** example of *exceptional test data* the programmer could use to test the program.   1

[Turn over

MARKS DO NOT WRITE IN THIS MARGIN

14. Employees can only access their company network if they enter a correct username and password. A validation program is being developed and will run each time an employee logs on.

An extract of pseudocode from the program is shown below.

```
Line 1  RECEIVE userName FROM (STRING) KEYBOARD
Line 2  RECEIVE pinNumber FROM (STRING) KEYBOARD
Line 3  IF userName VALID OR pinNumber VALID THEN
Line 4          Allow access to network
Line 5  ELSE
Line 6          SEND "Access Denied" TO SCREEN
Line 7  END IF
```

An error is noticed when the program is tested.

(a) Identify the line containing a logic error. 1

Line ______________________________

(b) State how this error should be corrected. 1

____

____

[Turn over for Question 15 on *Page eight*

DO NOT WRITE ON THIS PAGE

SECTION 2 — 70 marks

Attempt ALL questions

15. Holibobs sells holidays to its online customers. A page from Holibobs website is shown below.

(a) State the URL of this web page.   1

_____

MARKS | DO NOT WRITE IN THIS MARGIN

15. (continued)

(b) The webpage is created using HTML and Javascript.

   (i) State the feature of HTML code that allows the webpage to be formatted.

                                                1

   (ii) Clicking on the "Location Map" button opens the PlanetEarth Maps website in a new window.

     Explain why the HTML code for this link uses absolute addressing.   1

   (iii) The "weather widget" showing the current weather uses Javascript code.

     Suggest **one** other use of Javascript that could be added to this webpage.   1

(c) The Holibobs website includes a variety of media types which are stored using several standard file formats.

Complete the table below, indicating where the following file formats have been used on the website.

The first one has been done for you.   2

File format	Example
pdf	brochure
mp4	
jpeg	

[Turn over

MARKS

15. (continued)

(d) The photo gallery features a wide range of holiday images. A photograph is going to be added to the photo gallery.

Beach v1

  Preview

Item Type: JPEG colour image
Date taken: 28/07/2010
Dimensions: 4000x3000
Bit depth: 24bits
File size: 4.5MB

The file called Beach v1 was altered using graphic editing software and saved as a Beach v2.

Beach v2

✓ Preview

Item Type: JPEG colour image
Date taken: 28/07/2010
Dimensions: 4000x3000
Bit depth: 8bits
File size: 2.61MB

Explain why Beach v2 is being added to the photo gallery instead of Beach v1.

2

_____

_____

_____

MARKS

15. (continued)

(e) A search is carried out for holidays in Greece leaving from "Any London" airport after 1st May 2015.

Here are some of the matching holidays.

From	Resort	Departs	Price per person
Gatwick	Kefalonia	19/05/2015	£350·00
Gatwick	Corfu	30/05/2015	£325·00
Gatwick	Santorini	07/06/2015	£295·00
Luton	Zante	04/06/2015	£295·00
Stansted	Corfu	04/06/2015	£289·00
Stansted	Kefalonia	21/05/2015	£289·00
Gatwick	Kos	19/05/2015	£289·00
Luton	Halkidiki	03/06/2015	£250·00
Luton	Corfu	17/05/2015	£225·00
Stansted	Zante	28/05/2015	£225·00
Gatwick	Kos	12/06/2015	£199·00

Describe how the list is sorted.   2

_____

_____

_____

Total marks 10

[Turn over

MARKS | DO NOT WRITE IN THIS MARGIN

16. Jack has been asked to design a program to calculate the potential profit in a soft drink business. The program will store the costs involved in producing and selling one litre of each drink.

The following calculations will be used to output the profit made for each litre of drink.

Manufacturing Cost = Water Cost + Flavouring Cost + Labour Cost

Profit = Selling Price – Manufacturing Cost

(a) State the number of variables Jack would require in his program. **1**

_____

(b) Using pseudocode or a programming language of your choice, write a program to enter the required data, then calculate and display the profit for the soft drink business. **5**

Pseudocode ☐	OR	Programming Language ☐

MARKS

16. (continued)

(c) Jack adapts the program to ensure that **water cost** can only be entered as always greater than or equal to £0·10 and less than or equal to £0·50 per litre.

(i) State the standard algorithm that is used to ensure that data entered is acceptable.   1

_____

(ii) Complete the table below to show four different examples of test data for **water cost** and the type of each example.   3

Test Data	Type of Test Data
0·05	
0·45	normal
0·10	
	extreme

Total marks 10

[Turn over

MARKS

17. A supermarket website is used successfully by customers using desktop computers to order groceries online.

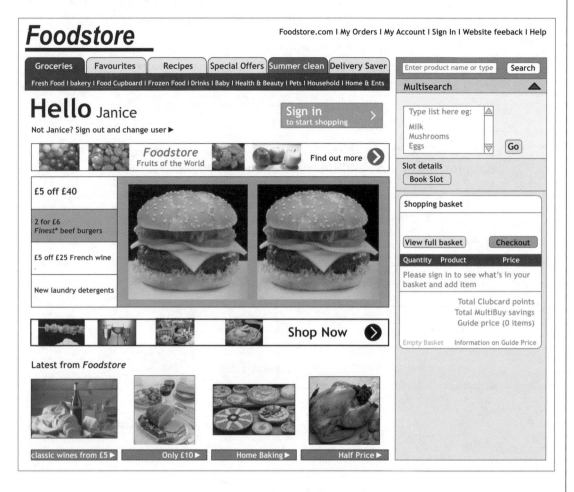

(a) The company has received complaints from some customers that the website is difficult to use on their tablet or smartphone.

Identify **two** reasons why the webpage above would be unsuitable for such portable devices.

2

Reason 1

_____

Reason 2

_____

(b) When buying items online, encryption is used. Explain why customers should be reassured by this feature.

1

_____

_____

MARKS | DO NOT WRITE IN THIS MARGIN

17. (continued)

(c) The supermarket is now developing a mobile application (app) for use on smartphones.

Explain why different types of smartphone would require different versions of the app.

1

_____

_____

(d) The mobile app contains a search page so that customers can find the items they want to buy from the supermarket.

Identify **two** smartphone input devices that would allow users to make use of the search features of this app.

2

_____

_____

[Turn over

MARKS

17. (continued)

(e) As well as having the mobile app and website the company provides a DVD of recipes.

Complete the table below to show which type of storage (magnetic, optical or solid state) is most appropriate for each of the following uses and why.

3

	Type of storage	Reason
Smartphone storing the app		
Web server storing the website		
Collection of video recipes stored on DVD		

(f) The minimum amount of RAM required to run the app is 1 Gigabyte.

State what RAM stands for.

1

_____

_____

Total marks 10

[Turn over for Question 18 on *Page eighteen*

DO NOT WRITE ON THIS PAGE

MARKS | DO NOT WRITE IN THIS MARGIN

18. An athlete is developing a mobile application (app).

The app will allow athletes to track weight in Kg.

Part of the pseudocode for this app is shown below.

```
......
.....
Line 15   SEND "Enter your new weight" TO DISPLAY
Line 16   RECEIVE newWeight FROM (REAL) KEYBOARD
Line 17      IF newWeight > previousWeight [counter] THEN
Line 18          SEND ["You have gained weight"] TO DISPLAY
Line 19      END IF
Line 20   SET previousWeight [counter] TO newWeight
....
.....
```

(a) (i) Identify the line that includes a condition.   1

Line _____

(ii) Identify the line that stores a value in an array.   1

Line _____

(iii) Identify the line that accepts input values into the program.   1

Line _____

(b) When the code for the program is written the programmer mis-types the word UNTIL, typing UNTOL instead.

State the type of programming error being described above.   1

_____

MARKS | DO NOT WRITE IN THIS MARGIN

18. (continued)

(c) The pseudocode is edited to ensure that the new weight being entered is acceptable.

```
....

Line 16    REPEAT

Line 17             RECEIVE newWeight FROM (REAL) KEYBOARD

Line 18    UNTIL newWeight > 20 AND newWeight < 70

......
```

(i) State the **type** of loop shown above.   1

_____

(ii) State an input **the use**r could enter to enable the program to continue from line 18.   1

_____

_____

(d) State another design notation that could have been used to design the app.   1

_____

(e) While the program is being implemented, the programmer stops occasionally to run the program.

State the type of translator you would recommend the programmer uses in this situation.

Explain your answer.   2

Translator _____

Explanation _____

_____

_____

_____

(f) State the component required to convert the data from the mobile devices touchscreen into data that can be used by the app.   1

_____

Total marks 10

MARKS

19. Ally has designed a website that encourages children to learn about energy saving and conservation.

    Ally plans to include 2 sections – a personal carbon footprint calculator and a game to play.

    (a) The carbon footprint calculator takes the user through a list of questions about their current energy usage.

    Here are Ally's designs for some of the questions.

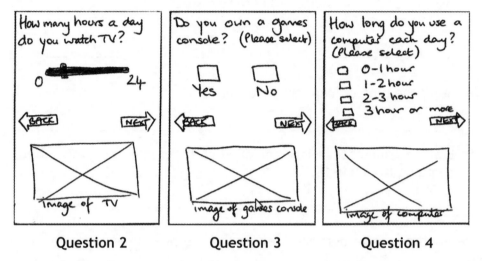

| Question 2 | Question 3 | Question 4 |

    (i) Referring to the designs above, draw a diagram to represent the navigation structure for the carbon footprint calculator.   2

MARKS | DO NOT WRITE IN THIS MARGIN

19. (a) (continued)

(ii) At the end of the questions, the user's carbon footprint is calculated.

Explain what is meant by a carbon footprint.

1

_____

_____

(iii) When Ally is testing the website, she notices that the total carbon footprint worked out is not calculated correctly.

Explain why this is a logic error and not a syntax error.

1

_____

_____

[Turn over

MARKS | DO NOT WRITE IN THIS MARGIN

19. (continued)

(b) In the game section of the website, players are shown a board with pairs of picture tiles placed randomly.

These are then flipped over to hide the images. Players have to flip two tiles trying to find two matching images until all pairs have been found.

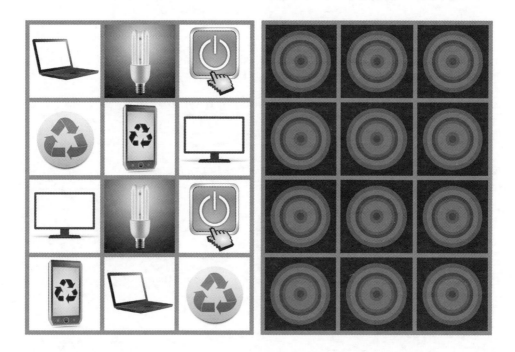

Images to be paired are displayed to user to be memorised	Tiles are then flipped to start the game

(i) Identify a situation in the game where Ally will need to implement the following programming constructs.

2

Selection	
Repetition	

MARKS | DO NOT WRITE IN THIS MARGIN

19. (b) (continued)

(ii) When a correct pair of images is found, a tip giving advice about energy use or conservation is displayed.

Write the **advice** that should be included with these images.   2

Image	Advice
	"Recycle your old mobile phone to keep hazardous waste out of landfill"

(iii) When creating the website, Ally copies images, sections of text and ideas from a website about energy use.

Explain why she might be in breach of the Copyright Designs and Patents Act.   1

_____

_____

(iv) When the website is released it has a pdf that can be downloaded free.

She has a wireless network available as well as her mobile phone network.

State **one** reason for selecting the wireless option to download the pdf.   1

_____

_____

Total marks 10

MARKS | DO NOT WRITE IN THIS MARGIN

20. A programming language provides the following pre-defined functions.

move(n)   n = distance moved in pixels

rotate(d)   d = degrees turned (positive means clockwise)

These can be used by the programmer to draw lines.

A programmer writes the code to draw a square. The code is shown below.

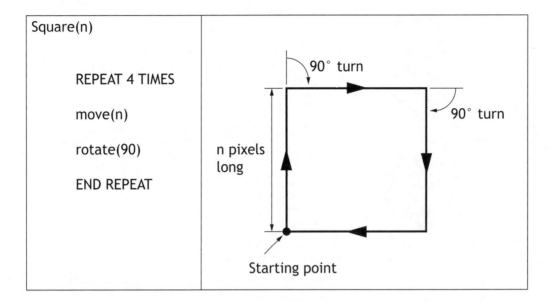

Square(n)

```
REPEAT 4 TIMES

move(n)

rotate(90)

END REPEAT
```

(a) Write the code that would draw a hexagon.   3

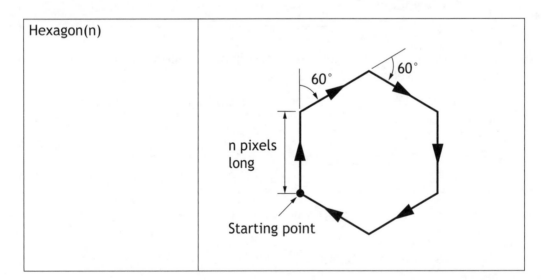

Hexagon(n)

(b) Describe one way you could make the programmer's code more readable.   1

_____

(c) Suggest a new pre-defined function that could be added to this programming language.   1

_____

MARKS | DO NOT WRITE IN THIS MARGIN

20. (continued)

(d) The following program uses the Square(n) function to draw a pattern.

Two values have been missed out from the code.

Complete the code by filling in the values in the two boxes. **2**

REPEAT [ ] TIMES

square(n)

rotate([ ])

END REPEAT

Direction of first move

Starting point

(e) The shapes that are drawn by the program can be saved as vector graphics.

Describe how a square would be saved as a vector graphic. **2**

_____

_____

(f) Every time a new function is added to the programming language it is designed using pseudocode.

State another design notation that could be used to design the new functions. **1**

_____

_____

Total marks **10**

[Turn over

MARKS | DO NOT WRITE IN THIS MARGIN

21. BigTech Gadgets are organising an exhibition to showcase cutting edge developments in technology. BigTech Gadgets want to store the details of products being demonstrated by companies.

Some sample data is shown in the table below.

Exhibitor Code	Company Name	Area	Stand Number	Product Reference	Item Name	Price (£)
SG100	FutureTech	Tech Zone	22	GD101	3D Printer	1245
SG100	FutureTech	Tech Zone	22	GD102	3D Printer XL	1699
SG176	Digital80	Photo Zone	49	GD208	360 Camera	800
SG203	TechATive	Active Zone	123	GD187	GoJet	1300
SG203	TechATive	Active Zone	123	GD324	RollerJet	500
SG489	ABCMusic	Music Zone	234	GD387	Xkey	350
SG489	ABCMusic	Music Zone	234	GD367	Xkey Plus	500
SG512	HitechGaming	Games Zone	288	GD654	HowPower2	149

(a) To avoid data duplication, a database with two linked tables is proposed – EXHIBITOR table and PRODUCT table.

   (i) List the fields/attributes that should be included in each table.   **2**

EXHIBITOR table	PRODUCT table

   (ii) Identify the foreign key used to link the two tables.   **1**

_____

(b) When implementing the database, BigTech Gadgets decide to include an image of each product.

Name the field **type** required to store an image.   **1**

_____

MARKS

21. (continued)

(c) The Stand Number **must** contain the number of the exhibition stand to be used by the company.

Name the type of validation that should be implemented on this field.   1

_____

(d) Visitors to the exhibition will be able to find information using an interactive touchscreen kiosk.

The kiosk includes a map with the location of each zone in the exhibition hall.

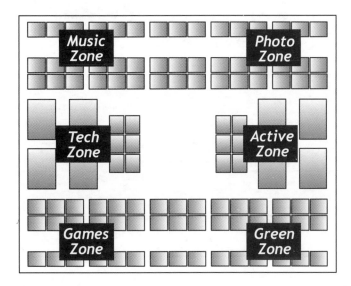

(i) Identify **one** feature that makes this a suitable user interface for a touchscreen kiosk.   1

_____

(ii) When the visitor selects the **tech zone button** on the kiosk, a list of companies exhibiting in that area is displayed.

Describe what happens within the database when this button is selected.   2

_____

_____

_____

_____

MARKS | DO NOT WRITE IN THIS MARGIN

21. (continued)

(e) Another screen from the kiosk is shown below.

Identify **two** features used on this screen to aid navigation.   2

_____

_____

Total marks 10

[END OF QUESTION PAPER]

MARKS | DO NOT WRITE IN THIS MARGIN

ADDITIONAL SPACE FOR ANSWERS

ADDITIONAL SPACE FOR ANSWERS

MARKS | DO NOT WRITE IN THIS MARGIN

Page thirty

NATIONAL 5

2015

N5

National Qualifications 2015

Mark

X716/75/01

Computing Science

WEDNESDAY, 6 MAY
9:00 AM – 10:30 AM

Fill in these boxes and read what is printed below.

Full name of centre

Town

Forename(s)

Surname

Number of seat

Date of birth
Day	Month	Year	Scottish candidate number

Total marks — 90

SECTION 1 — 20 marks

Attempt ALL questions.

SECTION 2 — 70 marks

Attempt ALL questions.

Show all working.

Write your answers clearly in the spaces provided in this booklet. Additional space for answers is provided at the end of this booklet. If you use this space you must clearly identify the question number you are attempting.

Use **blue** or **black** ink.

Before leaving the examination room you must give this booklet to the Invigilator; if you do not, you may lose all the marks for this paper.

SQA

MARKS | DO NOT WRITE IN THIS MARGIN

SECTION 1 — 20 MARKS

Attempt ALL Questions

1. Convert the decimal number 164 into the equivalent 8-bit binary number. **1**

2. A computer program is created to store data about the total number of pupils who pass an exam.

   State the most suitable data type for the total. **1**

3. The pseudocode shown below uses a simple condition.

   IF age < 5 THEN SEND nursery TO DISPLAY

   Create a complex condition that will display "school" if a person is between the ages of 5 and 18 inclusive. **2**

MARKS

4. A web browser keeps a history of websites visited. State **one** other feature of a web browser.

1

_____

_____

5. This pseudocode allows the user to guess the age of a teddy bear to win it in a competition.

Line 1	RECEIVE guess FROM (INTEGER) KEYBOARD
Line 2	WHILE guess < 1 OR guess > 80 DO
Line 3	SEND "invalid guess: please try again" TO DISPLAY
Line 4	RECEIVE guess FROM (INTEGER) KEYBOARD
Line 5	END WHILE

Complete the table below to show normal and exceptional test data for guess.

2

Type of Test Data	Test Data
normal	
exceptional	

[Turn over

MARKS | DO NOT WRITE IN THIS MARGIN

6. Kirsty is creating a website for a computer games company. Here is part of the page.

About Us   Contact Details   Online Store   **Vacancies**

Give **one** reason why the **design** of these links is not good practice.   1

_____

_____

7. Explain the purpose of lines 5 to 8 in this pseudocode.   2

```
...
Line 4      SET password TO "h1gh@sch00l"
Line 5      REPEAT
Line 6          SEND "Please enter your password" TO DISPLAY
Line 7          RECEIVE user_guess FROM (INTEGER) KEYBOARD
Line 8      UNTIL password = user_guess
```

_____

_____

_____

_____

MARKS

8. Explain why file compression is used before transferring files to cloud storage.

    1

_____

_____

_____

_____

9. Describe **two** methods of improving the readability of code.

    2

Method 1 _____

_____

_____

Method 2 _____

_____

_____

10. State the **data type** of the variable "password" in the code below.

    1

```
...
Line 12    SEND "Please enter your password" TO DISPLAY
Line 13    IF (password < > "h1gh@sch00l") THEN
Line 14            SEND "error: please re-enter password" TO DISPLAY
Line 15    END IF
```

_____

[Turn over

MARKS

11. Patryk is setting up a network for a school. Give **two** reasons why Patryk would choose a client/server network rather than a peer-to-peer network.   **2**

Reason 1 _____

_____

_____

Reason 2 _____

_____

_____

12. Katie is in her back garden using her smartphone to access her neighbour's wireless network. State the law Katie is breaking.   **1**

_____

13. Describe how **keylogging** can be an online security risk.   **1**

_____

_____

_____

_____

_____

_____

14. A company has both a wired and wireless network. The wireless network allows portability of workstations. Describe **one** advantage for the company of the wired network over the wireless network.   **1**

_____

_____

_____

_____

MARKS | DO NOT WRITE IN THIS MARGIN

15. All of the links in this information system have been tested.

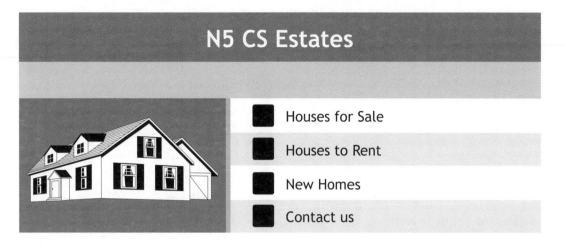

State **one** other type of testing that is used in this information system.   1

_____

_____

_____

[Turn over

SECTION 2 — 70 MARKS

Attempt ALL Questions

16. A retailer wants to set up a website to sell products online.

A template is selected which helps create the website by providing a ready-made structure as shown below.

(a) The template shown above provides consistency of font - colour, style and size of text.

Identify other features to aid good user interface design.

2

_____

_____

_____

_____

MARKS | DO NOT WRITE IN THIS MARGIN

Question 16 (continued)

(b) Once the website is created using the template, it is tested using a variety of browsers.

Explain why the webpages appear the same in each web browser.   1

_____

_____

_____

(c) Each web page requires an image of one of the products. A suitable photograph is taken with a digital camera and uploaded to a computer for editing.

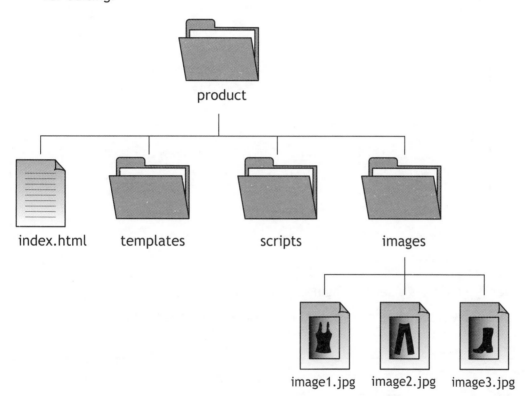

(i) A photograph for the homepage is stored in a folder called **images** as shown above.

The photograph is stored as **image1.jpg**. Name **one** other standard file format for graphics.   1

_____

(ii) State the type of addressing that should be used to include the file **image1.jpg** on the **index.html** page.   1

_____

MARKS | DO NOT WRITE IN THIS MARGIN

Question 16 (c) (continued)

(iii) The photograph, before editing, is 4 inch by 6 inch with a resolution of 600 dpi and 24-bit colour depth. Calculate the file size of the photograph.

State your answer using appropriate units. Show all your working.   **3**

(d) A website contains a search engine.

Explain how a search engine is used to produce a list of results.   **2**

_____

_____

_____

_____

_____

_____

MARKS | DO NOT WRITE IN THIS MARGIN

17. Pseudocode for a short program is written to calculate VAT on products. Part of the pseudocode is shown below.

```
...
Line 7    SET vatRate TO 0.2
Line 8    RECEIVE productCost FROM (REAL) KEYBOARD
Line 9    SET productVat TO productCost * vatRate
```

(a) Explain how the value in the variable productCost will be stored in the computer.

2

_____

_____

_____

_____

(b) The program is tested but stops running after a few lines. An error is highlighted.

   (i) Name the type of translator being used.

1

_____

   (ii) State **one** disadvantage of using this type of translator.

1

_____

_____

(c) When all errors are removed, the completed program is translated. A section of the translated code is shown below.

$$\begin{vmatrix} 1\,0\,1\,1\,0\,0\,0\,1 \\ 0\,0\,1\,0\,1\,1\,1\,0 \\ 1\,1\,1\,1\,0\,1\,0\,1 \\ 0\,1\,1\,0\,1\,1\,1\,0 \end{vmatrix}$$

State the type of programming language the code has been translated into.

1

_____

MARKS | DO NOT WRITE IN THIS MARGIN

Question 17 (continued)

(d) A diagram of a computer system is shown below.

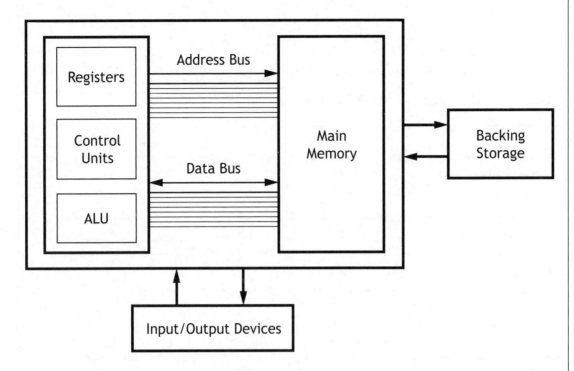

The following part of the program is executed.

...

Line 9   SET productVat TO productCost * vatRate

Name the part of the computer system that will carry out each of the following tasks during the execution of this line of code.

(i) Carries the location of productCost in main memory.   1

_____

(ii) Transfers the value of productCost from main memory to the processor.   1

_____

(iii) Performs the VAT calculation.   1

_____

MARKS | DO NOT WRITE IN THIS MARGIN

Question 17 (continued)

(e) The program is backed-up onto an external hard drive which is connected to the computer using an interface.

Describe **two** purposes of an interface.   2

Purpose 1 _____

_____

Purpose 2 _____

_____

[Turn over

MARKS | DO NOT WRITE IN THIS MARGIN

18. Here is the School Learner section of the Scottish Qualifications Authority (SQA) website.

(a) Describe one **purpose** of this section of the website.   1

_____

_____

_____

_____

(b) State the domain name of this webpage URL.   1

_____

(c) This web page design includes several features to aid accessibility.

   (i) Identify **one** of these features.   1

     _____

     _____

   (ii) Explain how this feature aids accessibility.   1

     _____

     _____

     _____

     _____

MARKS | DO NOT WRITE IN THIS MARGIN

Question 18 (continued)

(d) The HTML code used to include the SQA logo uses the *img src* tag shown below.

<img src= "../images/sqa-logo.gif">

Name the standard file format used to store the image.   **1**

_____

_____

(e) The web page includes the following navigation feature (breadcrumb).

✗ SQA Home > I am a... > Learner > **School learner**

Explain how this feature aids navigation.   **1**

_____

_____

_____

_____

_____

[Turn over

MARKS | DO NOT WRITE IN THIS MARGIN

Question 18 (continued)

(f) Sally uses the Exam Tools section to search for her own National 5 courses to build her own timetable and print the result.

List View	Calendar View			
Subject	**Qualification**	**Date**	**Time**	**?**
Italian	National 5	Thursday 30 April 2015	09:00–10:30	⊖
Italian	National 5	Thursday 30 April 2015	10:50–11:15	⊖
Graphic Communication	National 5	Thursday 30 April 2015	13:00–14:30	⊖
Computing Science	National 5	Wednesday 6 May 2015	09:00–10:30	⊖
Music	National 5	Friday 8 May 2015	13:00–13:45	⊖
English	National 5	Thursday 14 May 2015	09:00–10:00	⊖
English	National 5	Thursday 14 May 2015	10:20–11:50	⊖
Art and Design	National 5	Friday 29 May 2015	13:30–14:40	⊖

📇 Export to iCal   🖨 Print   ✉ Email my Timetable

Subject
Graphic Communication ▼

Qualification
National 5 ▼

Search

Circle **one** example on the webpage above that might make use of Javascript.

1

(g) Describe how the personal National 5 timetable results have been sorted.

2

_____

_____

_____

_____

MARKS | DO NOT WRITE IN THIS MARGIN

Question 18 (continued)

(h) Sally downloads a past paper from another area of the website.

Describe **one** concern that Sally might have when she downloads a past paper.

1

_____

_____

_____

_____

[Turn over

MARKS | DO NOT WRITE IN THIS MARGIN

19. A program is written to calculate the cost of feeding chickens for one month. Chickens eat 5 Kilograms of grain each month. An incomplete design for the program is shown below.

Line 1	SEND "Enter the number of chickens and the cost of grain" TO DISPLAY
Line 2	RECEIVE numberOfChickens FROM (_____) KEYBOARD
Line 3	RECEIVE pricePerKilo FROM (_____) KEYBOARD
Line 4	SEND "Is the grain full price?" TO DISPLAY
Line 5	RECEIVE fullPrice FROM (_____) KEYBOARD
Line 6	IF fullPrice = True THEN
Line 7	SET totalPrice TO numberOfChickens *5*pricePerKilo
Line 8	END IF
Line 9	IF fullPrice = False THEN
Line 10	SET totalPrice TO numberOfChickens *5*(pricePerKilo*0.8)
Line 11	END IF
Line 12	SEND ["The total cost of grain required for" & numberOfChickens & "chickens is £" & totalPrice] TO DISPLAY

(a) The above design should show the type of data being entered by keyboard in Lines 2, 3 and 5. State the most appropriate data types for the following variables. 3

numberOfChickens _____

pricePerKilo _____

fullPrice _____

MARKS

Question 19 (continued)

(b)   (i)   State the lines of pseudocode that contain conditional statements.   2

_____

_____

    (ii)   State the part of the processor that compares the values in a conditional statement.   1

_____

(c)   The program is later improved to store the totalPrice for each month of a year.

   (i)   State the data structure that would be required to store the list of totalPrice values.   2

_____

_____

   (ii)   State the **type** of loop required to repeat the code in lines 1 to 12 for each month of the year. Explain why this type of loop would be used.   2

Type of Loop _____

Explanation _____

_____

_____

[Turn over

MARKS | DO NOT WRITE IN THIS MARGIN

20. A supermarket has a flat file database storing information about the 20,000 products it stocks. Part of the database is shown below.

Dept ID	Dept Name	Department Manager	Product Code	Product Type	Product Name
4	Toiletries	H Green	100356	Toothpaste	Dentasparkle
10	Dry Goods	A Ahmed	204672	Cereal	Oatycrunch
6	Cleaning Products	F McMaster	318410	Shoe Polish	Shine
10	Dry Goods	A Ahmed	396039	Packet Soup	Mug-o-Soup
10	Dry Goods	A Ahmed	401284	Biscuits	Choco Snaps
4	Toiletries	H Green	672936	Shower Gel	Clean & Fresh
6	Cleaning Products	F McMaster	324221	Wipes	GermGo

(a) The design structure of the database looks like this.

Field Name	Field Type	Field Size	Validation
Dept ID	Number	2	>0 and <11
Dept Name	Text	20	
Department Manager	Text	20	
Product Code	Text	6	Required
Product Type	Text	20	
Product Name	Text	20	

Name **two** types of *validation* that could be applied to the field **Product Code**.   2

Validation 1 _____

Validation 2 _____

(b) The supermarket decides to change the name of the "Cleaning Products" department to "Household Products". Describe a potential problem when changing this data in a *flat file* database design.   1

_____

_____

_____

_____

MARKS | DO NOT WRITE IN THIS MARGIN

Question 20 (continued)

(c) A decision is made to modify the design of the database to *linked tables* with two tables: DEPARTMENT and PRODUCT.   Each table will have a *primary key*.

    (i)   State the purpose of a primary key.   **1**

_____

_____

_____

    (ii)   Identify a suitable primary key for each table.   **2**

        DEPARTMENT _____

        PRODUCT   _____

(d)   Three new fields

Product In Stock, Product Picture and Product Price

are to be inserted into the PRODUCT table as shown below.

Product Code	Product Type	Product Name	Product in Stock	Product Picture	Product Price
100356	Toothpaste	Dentasparkle	True		1·99
204672	Cereal	Oatycrunch	False		2·45

Name a suitable *field type* for the following new fields.   **2**

Product In Stock _____

Product Picture _____

[Turn over

MARKS | DO NOT WRITE IN THIS MARGIN

Question 20 (continued)

(e) The supermarket decides to replace its current computers.

Explain **two** ways the company should dispose of the "old" computer systems.

2

_____

_____

_____

_____

_____

_____

_____

[Turn over for Question 21 on *Page twenty-four*

DO NOT WRITE ON THIS PAGE

MARKS | DO NOT WRITE IN THIS MARGIN

21. A program is required to calculate the quantity of bricks required to build a wall. The program will ask the user to enter the dimensions of the wall and a single brick. 1 cm will be added onto the dimensions of the brick to allow for mortar between the bricks. Area of a rectangle is calculated by multiplying the length by height.

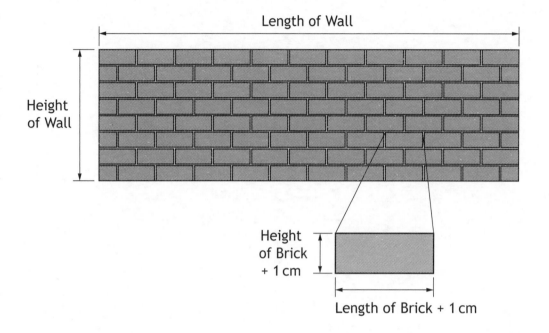

A design for the program is shown below.

Line 1	RECEIVE lengthOfWall FROM (REAL) KEYBOARD
Line 2	RECEIVE heightOfWall FROM (REAL) KEYBOARD
Line 3	RECEIVE lengthOfBrick FROM (REAL) KEYBOARD
Line 4	RECEIVE heightOfBrick FROM (REAL) KEYBOARD
Line 5	SET lengthOfBrick TO lengthOfBrick + 1
Line 6	SET heightOfBrick TO heightOfBrick + 1
Line 7	<calculate the quantity of bricks needed>
Line 8	SEND ["The number of bricks needed is –" numberOfBricks] TO DISPLAY

MARKS | DO NOT WRITE IN THIS MARGIN

Question 21 (continued)

(a) A brick length must be greater than 15 and less than 50.

Using pseudocode or a programming language of your choice, show how input validation could be used to ensure a valid brick length is entered by the user.

3

Pseudocode [ ]   OR Programming Language [   ]

(b) Using the information obtained in Lines 1 to 6.

Use pseudocode or a programming language of your choice to show how Line 7 would be implemented.

4

Pseudocode [ ]   OR Programming Language [   ]

MARKS | DO NOT WRITE IN THIS MARGIN

Question 21 (continued)

(c) The program is tested and gives the following output.

The number of bricks needed is: 345.32

The number of bricks needing to be ordered is 346.

Describe how a pre-defined function could be used to ensure that the correct number of bricks is ordered.

2

_____

_____

_____

_____

_____

(d) Mortar is required to hold the bricks in place. The following calculation will be used to calculate the amount of mortar required.

Mortar = (2 * sand) + cement + water

State the number of variables required.

1

_____

MARKS | DO NOT WRITE IN THIS MARGIN

22. Maggie has just started her own photography business taking pictures at weddings and party events. She uses her digital camera with a different 64 Gigabyte memory card for each event.

   (a) The memory card in the camera is an example of solid state storage. Explain why this is more suitable for a digital camera than magnetic storage.   **2**

   _____

   _____

   _____

   (b) If a photograph file is 25 Megabytes in size, calculate how many photos Maggie can take at each event before her memory card is full.

   Show your working.   **2**

   Maggie transfers the photos to her tablet before the end of each event so that guests can browse the images and then place orders to buy copies.

   (c) Describe **two** advantages of using a tablet rather than a laptop computer for this task.   **2**

   Advantage 1 _____

   _____

   Advantage 2 _____

   _____

MARKS | DO NOT WRITE IN THIS MARGIN

Question 22 (continued)

Maggie discovers that using one tablet restricts the number of guests who can view the images during the event and as a result, she does not make many sales.

(d) Maggie decides to use an app called SnapsGalore with cloud storage to organise and manage her photos.

SnapsGalore

Unlimited cloud storage

- No more storage capacity problems
- Unlimited secure storage
- Automatic backup
- Multiple login options
- Cross platform OS compatibility
- Searchable database automatically created when you upload

(i) Describe how cloud storage can be used to provide wider access to the photos.

1

_____

_____

_____

_____

(ii) Identify the feature of the app that allows guests to access the photos even though they have different types of devices.

1

_____

_____

MARKS | DO NOT WRITE IN THIS MARGIN

Question 22 (continued)

(e) Maggie uses the free wireless (WiFi) connection in the venue to transfer the images from the tablet to the SnapsGalore server.

Describe **two** concerns she may have about using the WiFi connection.　2

Concern 1 _____

_____

_____

Concern 2 _____

_____

_____

[END OF QUESTION PAPER]

MARKS

DO NOT
WRITE IN
THIS
MARGIN

ADDITIONAL SPACE FOR ANSWERS

MARKS | DO NOT WRITE IN THIS MARGIN

ADDITIONAL SPACE FOR ANSWERS

[BLANK PAGE]

DO NOT WRITE ON THIS PAGE

NATIONAL 5

2016

N5

National Qualifications 2016

Mark

X716/75/01

Computing Science

FRIDAY, 27 MAY

1:00 PM — 2:30 PM

Fill in these boxes and read what is printed below.

Full name of centre

Town

Forename(s)

Surname

Number of seat

Date of birth

Day	Month	Year	Scottish candidate number

Total marks — 90

SECTION 1 — 20 marks

Attempt ALL questions.

SECTION 2 — 70 marks

Attempt ALL questions.

Show all working.

Write your answers clearly in the spaces provided in this booklet. Additional space for answers is provided at the end of this booklet. If you use this space you must clearly identify the question number you are attempting.

Use **blue** or **black** ink.

Before leaving the examination room you must give this booklet to the Invigilator; if you do not, you may lose all the marks for this paper.

MARKS | DO NOT WRITE IN THIS MARGIN

SECTION 1 – 20 MARKS

Attempt ALL Questions

1. Convert the decimal value 227 into the equivalent 8-bit binary number.   **1**

2. Explain why it is important that program code is readable.   **1**

_____

_____

3. Explain why a **database** should not be stored in ROM memory.   **1**

_____

_____

_____

_____

MARKS | DO NOT WRITE IN THIS MARGIN

4. Give **one** reason for using this type of selection.

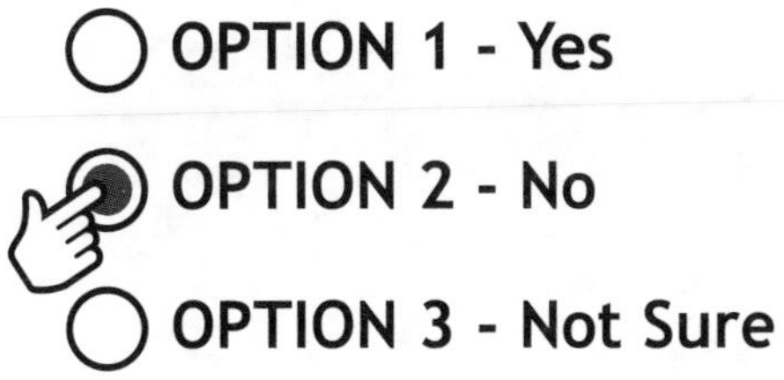

⚪ **OPTION 1 - Yes**

🔘 **OPTION 2 - No**

⚪ **OPTION 3 - Not Sure**

1

_____

_____

_____

_____

5. State the function of a processor's registers.   1

_____

_____

[Turn over

MARKS | DO NOT WRITE IN THIS MARGIN

6. Anti-virus software may be included in a security suite.

State **two** other types of software which should be included in a security suite.

2

1 _____

_____

2 _____

_____

7. Criminals can steal your identity by using keylogger programs. State **two** other ways in which identity theft can be carried out.

2

1 _____

_____

2 _____

_____

MARKS | DO NOT WRITE IN THIS MARGIN

8. A novice is one type of user of an information system.

   State **one** other type of user.   1

   _____

9. This code design monitors the temperature of food as it is reheated.

   Line 1   RECEIVE temperature FROM (REAL) *<temperature sensor>*

   Line 2   WHILE temperature < 82 DO

   Line 3   SEND "temperature too low: continue to reheat" TO DISPLAY

   Line 4   RECEIVE temperature FROM (REAL) *<temperature sensor>*

   Line 5   END WHILE

   Explain what will happen in lines 2 to 5 if the sensor detects 63°.   2

   _____

   _____

   _____

   _____

   _____

   _____

   _____

10. Lucy is looking for a summer holiday on-line. She wishes to leave on 22nd July from her local airport, and early in the afternoon.

    State which database operation is being carried out as she uses the website.   1

    _____

MARKS | DO NOT WRITE IN THIS MARGIN

11. Translators are used to convert high level languages into machine code.

Identify each type of translator.

	Type of Translator
This translator program reports errors at the end of translation.	
This translator needs to be present in memory each time the program is executed.	

2

12. A running group has 16 members. They are taking part in a marathon.

Using pseudocode or a programming language of your choice, write the code which will take in each runner's time for the marathon.

2

MARKS | DO NOT WRITE IN THIS MARGIN

13. Before launching the website below, it is tested. The testers complain about the effectiveness of the website's navigation.

Identify **two** examples of poor navigation, stating what could be done to improve the situation.   2

1 _____

_____

_____

_____

2 _____

_____

_____

_____

14. State the **type** of network which has no centralised storage.   1

_____

[Turn over

SECTION 2 — 70 MARKS

Attempt ALL Questions

15. FlightCrazy is a new company offering a flight booking service to business customers. They want to set up a database to store flight details. A researcher starts to gather information from airport timetables about available flight times.

Route ID	Departure Airport	Destination Airport	Day	Departure Time	Duration (hrs)	Airline Ref	Airline Name	Flight Number	Aircraft Code
001	Edinburgh	Amsterdam	Monday	07:00	01:35	KL	KLM	KL1276	737
001	Edinburgh	Amsterdam	Monday	08:00	01:30	U2	Easyjet	U26921	319
001	Edinburgh	Amsterdam	Saturday	10:15	01:30	U2	Easyjet	U26921	320
001	Edin	Amsterdam	Monday	11:10	01:30	KL	KLM	KL1280	737
001	Edinburgh	Ams	Tuesday	07:00	01:35	KL	KLM	KL1276	737
003	Edinburgh	London Heathrow	Monday	08:00	01:35	BA	British Airways	BA1461	EQV
002	Edinburgh	London Gatwick	Mon	06:40	01:35	BA	British Airways	BA2931	EQV
002	Edin	London GAT	Sat	06:25	01:30	U2	Easyjet	U2802	EQV
003	Edinburgh	Heathrow	Monday	09:10	01:30	VS	Virgin Atlantic	VS3002	320

(a) If the full database is created as a flat file, explain why "RouteID" is not a suitable primary key for the table.   1

_____

_____

MARKS | DO NOT WRITE IN THIS MARGIN

15.   **(continued)**

(b)   Describe **two** problems in creating this as a flat file database.   2

Problem 1

_____

_____

_____

Problem 2

_____

_____

_____

(c)   FlightCrazy decided that using a flat file database is not suitable.
State a more suitable type of database.   1

_____

(d)   State the **field type** that should be used for "Aircraft Code".   1

_____

[Turn over

15. (continued)

(e) During the development of this database the following input form is created.

```
┌──────────────────────────────────────────────┐
│ Search for a flight                            │
│                                                │
│   Departure Airport *    [Edinburgh        ▼]  │
│   Destination Airport *   Edinburgh            │
│                           Glasgow              │
│   ◉ One way    ○ Return   Aberdeen             │
│                           Dundee               │
│                           Inverness            │
│   Departure time          Wick                 │
│                                                │
│   Date of travel *       [            ]        │
│                                                │
│   Number of travellers * [            ] (max 6)│
│                                                │
│          [     Find Flights     ]              │
│                                                │
│      * indicates field cannot be left empty    │
└──────────────────────────────────────────────┘
```

(i) State **one** suitable type of validation for the Departure Airport field.   **1**

_____

(ii) Complete the table below to show suitable data values to test the Number of travellers field.   **2**

Type of Test data	Test data
Exceptional	
Extreme	

MARKS | DO NOT WRITE IN THIS MARGIN

15.　(continued)

(f)　During the testing of the completed database all the flights from Glasgow to all airports in London on the 8th June were found. The following output was produced.

11 flights match your search criteria				
From:	Glasgow	To:	London	
Date:	8th June			

Depart	Destination	Journey Time	Price	Airline
21:20	LTN	1h10	39	Easyjet
21:45	LGW	1h25	39	Easyjet
20:45	STN	1h20	40	Ryanair
06:30	STN	1h15	47	Easyjet
19:55	STN	1h15	47	Easyjet
21:00	LHR	1h15	47	British Airways
07:00	LTN	1h10	57	Easyjet
07:05	STN	1h20	57	Ryanair
09:20	LTN	1h10	57	Easyjet
10:25	STN	1h15	57	Ryanair
09:25	LGW	1h25	73	British Airways

Describe how the above results have been sorted.　　2

_____

_____

_____

[Turn over

MARKS | DO NOT WRITE IN THIS MARGIN

16. A Maths game is designed for primary school pupils to test number ordering. In the game the pupil is asked to enter two integer numbers. A third integer number is then randomly generated and shown to the user.

The user must then state if the random number is:

lower (l) than the two entered numbers
higher (h) than the two entered numbers
in the middle (m) of the two entered numbers.

A design for the code is shown below.

Line 1   *<enter the first number and assign to numOne>*
Line 2   *<enter the second number and assign to numTwo>*
Line 3   *<generate random number and assign to randNum>*
Line 4   SEND randNum TO DISPLAY
Line 5   RECEIVE guess FROM (CHARACTER) KEYBOARD
Line 6   IF guess = "l" AND randNum < numOne THEN
Line 7   SEND "Correct it is lower" TO DISPLAY
Line 8   SET score TO score + 1
Line 9   END IF
Line 10   IF guess = "m" AND randNum >= numOne AND randNum <= numTwo
Line 11   SEND "Correct it is in the middle" TO DISPLAY
Line 12   SET score TO score + 1
Line 13   END IF
Line 14   IF guess = "h" AND randNum > numTwo
Line 15   SEND "Correct it is higher" TO DISPLAY
Line 16   SET score TO score + 1
Line 17   END IF
Line 18   *<display incorrect message>*

(a) When the two numbers are entered the program should ensure that numTwo is always a higher number than numOne.

Using pseudocode or a programming language of your choice, write several lines to represent this input validation for line 2.   4

MARKS | DO NOT WRITE IN THIS MARGIN

16. **(continued)**

(b) When the pupil enters the answer it is stored in a variable called "guess".

State the **data type** stored by the variable "guess".   1

_____

(c) The program is run with the following data.

Variables	Values
numOne	7
numTwo	15
randNum	10
guess	m

State the output from the program.   1

_____

_____

_____

_____

(d) The program will have to make use of a pre-defined function.

State the pre-defined function used and describe its purpose.   2

_____

_____

(e) Using line numbers, describe how the code could be adapted, allowing the user to play the game 10 times using the same values for numOne and numTwo but a different random number each time.   2

_____

_____

_____

_____

_____

MARKS | DO NOT WRITE IN THIS MARGIN

17. John has been asked to design a website to promote an event being held to raise money for charity.

The organisers of the event provide this diagram showing the pages required and how they should be organised.

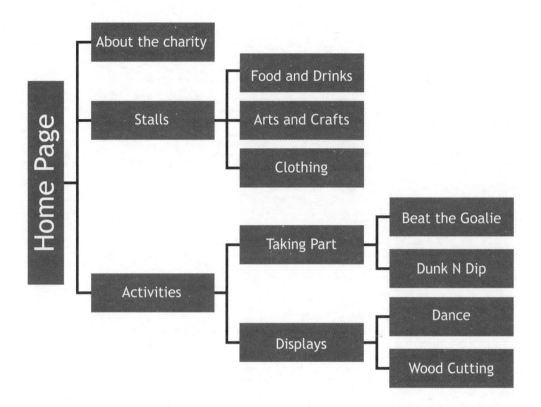

(a) What **type** of navigation structure is required for the website?   1

_____

_____

(b) State a design notation that John could use to design the layout of the pages.   1

_____

_____

(c) The homepage contains hyperlinks. Describe the function of a hyperlink.   1

_____

_____

_____

17.   (continued)

(d) John begins to build the website and stores all the files and resources on his hard disk.

Here is the file structure for the website.

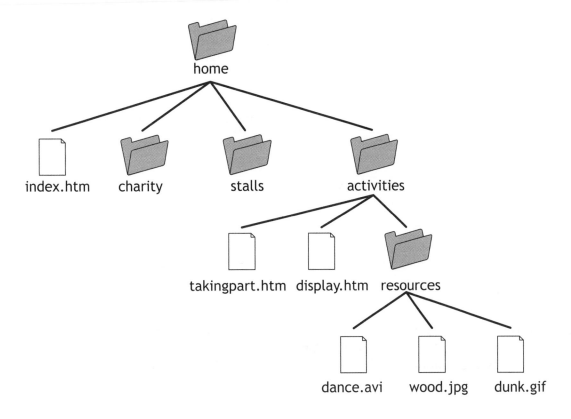

	MARKS	DO NOT WRITE IN THIS MARGIN

(i) State the type of data you would expect to be stored in the dance.avi file.   **1**

_____

(ii) State the **relative** address John should enter on the display.htm page to link to dunk.gif.   **1**

_____

_____

[Turn over

MARKS | DO NOT WRITE IN THIS MARGIN

17.   (continued)

(e)   John wants to include an external link to the charity and asks the event organisers to find out the URL.

(i)   Explain what is meant by an external link.   1

_____

_____

_____

_____

(ii)   State what the letters URL stand for.   1

U _____

R _____

L _____

(iii) The organisers give John a photograph file from the charity which measures 5 inches by 7 inches with a resolution of 600dpi and 24-bit colour depth. Calculate the storage required for the photograph.

State your answer using appropriate units. Show all your working.   3

MARKS | DO NOT WRITE IN THIS MARGIN

18. A software development company decides to review staff knowledge of computer related legislation.

Mikal is asked to create an app covering a range of legal issues.

(a) When Mikal records an introduction using audio software, he is prompted to select the sample rate.

Select sampling rate:

○   22050 Hz
○   44100 Hz
○   96000 Hz

(i) Describe the effect on the size of the sound file if the highest sample rate is selected.   1

_____

_____

_____

(ii) After recording, Mikal exports the file as a compressed file.

State a suitable standard file format he may have used.   1

_____

[Turn over

18.   **(continued)**

(b)   Mikal develops an interactive quiz for the app to test the staff's knowledge of legislation. The first question is about this recent article from a newspaper.

(i)   State the offence that has been committed under the Computer Misuse Act in this article.

1

_____

_____

(ii)   Describe another offence under the terms of this Act.

1

_____

_____

_____

MARKS | DO NOT WRITE IN THIS MARGIN

18.   (continued)

(c)   The next question that Mikal creates for the quiz is about another article.

Name the law which may have been broken in this case.   1

_____

_____

[Turn over

MARKS | DO NOT WRITE IN THIS MARGIN

18.   (continued)

(d) In line with Health and Safety legislation, the company provides adjustable seating and guidelines on maintaining good posture.

Mikal finds graphics on a website that he can use to illustrate his next quiz question.

A   B

C   D

(i) Explain why he might need to seek permission to use the graphics legally.   1

_____

_____

MARKS | DO NOT WRITE IN THIS MARGIN

18. (d) (continued)

(ii) Mikal uses the graphics to create question 3 for the app.

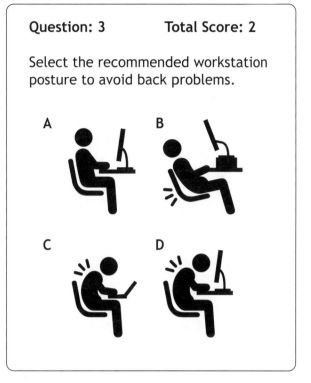

Question: 3   Total Score: 2

Select the recommended workstation posture to avoid back problems.

A   B

C   D

Using pseudocode or a programming language of your choice, write the code to show how the total score is calculated when the user answers question 3 correctly.   2

MARKS | DO NOT WRITE IN THIS MARGIN

18.   (continued)

(e) When the staff member runs the finished quiz, the app sends their details and their total score to a database file.

State **two** rights that the staff member has under the Data Protection Act with regard to their own data.

2

_____

_____

_____

_____

_____

MARKS | DO NOT WRITE IN THIS MARGIN

19. Gillian designs a program to calculate how much it costs to get her dog Penny groomed. The design is shown below.

Line 1   SET total = 0
Line 2   DECLARE all costs INITIALLY [35.00, 36.00, 40.00, 35.00, 42.50]
Line 3   FOR EACH cost FROM all costs DUE
Line 4   SET total=total+cost
Line 5   END FOR EACH
Line 6   SEND "The total cost = £"&total TO DISPLAY

(a) Describe the data structure that has been used to store the individual costs.   2

_____

_____

(b) Gillian writes and tests her program. It works perfectly calculating a correct total of 188.50.

   (i) With reference to line numbers, explain how the program calculates the final total.   3

_____

_____

_____

_____

_____

_____

   (ii) Describe how the contents of the variable total would be stored in the computer's memory.   2

_____

_____

[Turn over

MARKS | DO NOT WRITE IN THIS MARGIN

19.   (b)   (continued)

(iii)   Gillian edits the program with the following data:
[35.00, 36.00, 40.00, 35.00, 42.50, **45.00**]
The output is still 188.50.

A   Explain why the output is still 188.50.   1

_____

B   State how this error could be corrected.   1

_____

(c)   Concatenation has been used in line 6.

State the purpose of concatenation.   1

_____

_____

_____

[Turn over for next question

DO NOT WRITE ON THIS PAGE

MARKS | DO NOT WRITE IN THIS MARGIN

20. Sue uses a website called "Check your Defences!" to learn more about keeping her computer and data safe.

(a) Explain the purpose of a firewall.

1

_____

_____

(b) Explain how encryption can help keep data safe.

2

_____

_____

_____

_____

_____

_____

MARKS | DO NOT WRITE IN THIS MARGIN

20. **(continued)**

When Sue tries to download the mobile app onto her tablet PC, she gets the following message:

 This app is incompatible with your device

Check your Defences!
System requirements
Android 4·4 or higher
1·6 GHz
2Gb RAM
32 GB

She checks the specification for her tablet PC.

> Size: 267 x 187 x 8 mm
> Weight: 0·65 kg
> 1·83 GHz/2 GB RAM/16 GB
> Battery life: up to 8 hours
> Display: 8·3" full HD, 10 point multi-touch
> Operating system: Android 4·1
> USB 3·0, micro HDMI, microSD card slot
> 3·5 MP camera
> Microphone
> Stereo speakers
> Headphone jack
> Wi-Fi

(c) (i) Sue's tablet has a range of input and output devices. Identify **one** of each of these items on Sue's tablet.　　2

Input device _____

_____

Output device _____

_____

(ii) Identify **one** interface type on Sue's tablet.　　1

Interface type _____

_____

MARKS | DO NOT WRITE IN THIS MARGIN

20. **(c)** **(continued)**

(iii) Describe **one** function of an interface.   **1**

_____

_____

_____

(iv) Give **two** reasons why the app is incompatible with Sue's tablet PC.   **2**

Reason 1 _____

_____

_____

Reason 2 _____

_____

_____

MARKS | DO NOT WRITE IN THIS MARGIN

20. **(continued)**

(d) Sue's friend Jack views the website on his smart phone but the home screen looks different to the desktop version Sue had been using.

Smartphone version   Desktop version

Describe **one** reason why the user interface on the smartphone version is designed differently to the version Sue had used on her desktop.   1

_____

_____

_____

[Turn over

MARKS | DO NOT WRITE IN THIS MARGIN

21. A software developer is creating an online booking system for a bowling alley. Customers can book a bowling lane for a maximum of 4 people playing a maximum of 3 games.

The developer has used a flow chart to produce the program design. Part of the design is shown below.

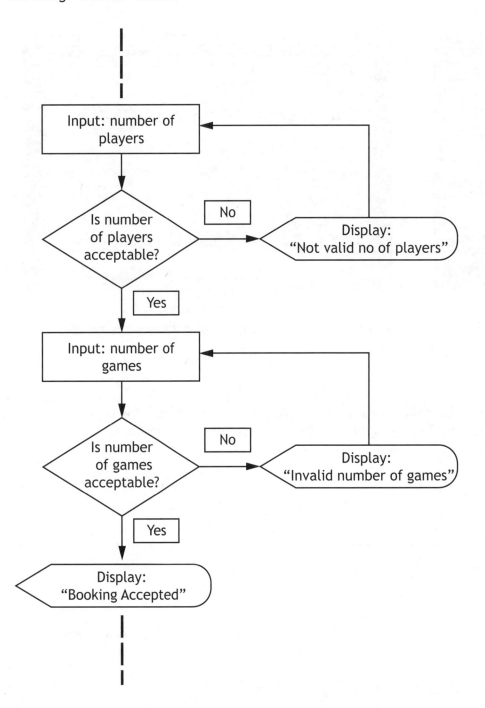

(a) (i) State **one** benefit of using the design notation shown above instead of pseudocode.

1

_____

_____

MARKS | DO NOT WRITE IN THIS MARGIN

21. (a) (continued)

(ii) Name the algorithm illustrated in the bowling alley program design.   **1**

_____

_____

(b)

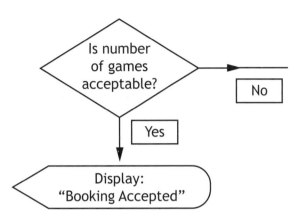

Using pseudocode or a programming language of your choice, complete the conditional statement at Line 3 below to implement this section of the design.   **3**

Line 3 _____ numPlayers _____ and

numGames _____

Line 4 SEND "Booking Accepted" TO DISPLAY

(c) The program is tested using a set of test data.

(i) Complete the table below to show three examples of test data types and the expected result for each type.   **3**

Test data	Test data type	Expected Result
numPlayers = 3 numGames = 2	Normal	Booking accepted
numPlayers = 4 numGames = 3		Booking accepted
numPlayers = 6 numGames = 3		

MARKS | DO NOT WRITE IN THIS MARGIN

21. (c) (continued)

(ii) The character "£" is entered as a test value for the number of players. This causes the program to crash.

State the **type** of error that would cause this crash. 1

_~~~~~~~~~~~~~_ ~~~~~

_~~~~~~~~~~~~~_ Run-time

(d) Error detection and correction in a program is easier if the code is readable.

State **one** technique that can be used to ensure *readability* of code. 1

_~~~~~~~~~~~~_ Internal commentary

Indentation   Meaningful variable names

[END OF QUESTION PAPER]

MARKS

ADDITIONAL SPACE FOR ANSWERS

MARKS | DO NOT WRITE IN THIS MARGIN

ADDITIONAL SPACE FOR ANSWERS

NATIONAL 5

Answers

SQA NATIONAL 5
COMPUTING SCIENCE 2016

NATIONAL 5 COMPUTING SCIENCE 2014

Section 1

1. *Explain:*
   An internal hyperlink points to a file/another page within a website
   An external hyperlink points to another website

2. *Name:* Browser

3. *Calculate:*
   400 × 600 × 8 =1920000 (bits)

   1920000/8 = 240000 (bytes)
   240000 (bytes)/1024
   = 234.375 (Kb)

4. *Name:* Arithmetic Logic Unit/ALU

5. *Convert:* 00101111

6. *State any one from:*
   - Data duplication
   - Data inconsistency or update/deletion/insertion anomalies
   - Data integrity errors (due to data inconsistency)
   - Inconsistent search results in multi-value fields

7. *Identify any one from:*
   - Encryption
   - Password/PIN
   - Biometric

8. *State any one from:*
   - Reduces the chance of human error
   - Does not require the user to type a text response
   - Speeds up the ordering process as inputs are reduced to mouse clicks
   - Allows the use of a touchscreen
   - Do not have to remember any types of pizza on offer

9. *Describe:*
   - Check navigation
   - Check all hyperlinks/hotspots
   - Ensure graphics are not pixelated
   - Ensure audio clips run
   - Any JavaScript issues
   - Check compatibility with browsers

10. *State any one from:*
    - Can access data from any computer device remotely
    - No requirement for own servers
    - Less need for own technical support on site
    - Automatic backup/recovery of data

11. *State any one from each list:*
    Client Server
    - Data can be stored/accessed centrally
    - Only accessible by registered users
    - Different access rights for users
    - Shared peripherals
    - Expensive with explanation

    Peer to Peer
    - Resources stored on device available to other peers
    - No centralised stored
    - Not as secure as Client Server
    - Risk from viruses

12. *Explain:*
    Line 2: Value stored in variable level (12) is outwith range, so loop implemented
    Line 3: Message sent to display
    Line 4: New value entered

13. An example of:
    - Non-numeric
    - Out of range
    - Real numbers

14. (a) Line 3

    (b) Replace OR with AND

Section 2

15. (a) *State:*
    http://www.holibobs.co.uk/greece/crete234.html

    (b) *State:*
    (i) Tags
        Styles

    (ii) *Explain:*
        External link to another site/server

    (iii) Any acceptable use of Javascript to create interactivity or dynamic content on this webpage

    (c) • mp4 – 'Download Videos' or 'Virtual Tour of Property' buttons
        • jpeg – Any example of a graphic on page or 'Photo Gallery' or 'Location Map' or 'Villa picture' or 'Holibobs Icon' or 'Weather Widget'

    (d) *Explain:*
        - Reduced colour depth
        - Smaller file size
        - Allows image to load faster

    (e) • Price descending
        • Resort ascending

16. (a) *State:*
    6

    (b) *Candidate answer must include:*
    4 values input – Water Cost, Flavour Cost, Labour Cost, Selling Price

    Manufacturing Cost = Water Cost + Flavouring Cost + Labour

    Profit = Selling Price – Manufacturing Cost

    Output of Profit

    (c) (i) *State:*
        (Input) Validation

    (ii)

Test Data (Flavouring)	Type of Test Data
0.05	exceptional
0.45	normal
0.10	extreme
0.50	extreme

17. (a) *Answers should identify parts of **this** webpage which will not be suitable on a small screen device.*
    For example:
    - Navigation bar does not fit across small screen
    - Too many columns
    - Too much information for small screen
    - Icons too small to click on right hand side
    - Would take too long to load images on portable device

(b) *Explain:*
    Personal details transmitted in code cannot be read (by hackers)
    OR
    Keeps personal data secure/safe
    OR
    Only the company can access the encrypted data

(c) *Explain:*
    Different operating systems on devices
    OR
    Hardware differences (resolution, dual core processor, memory etc)

(d) *Identify any two from:*
    - Touchscreen
    - Microphone
    - Camera

(e) *Complete the table:*
    Smartphone
    Storage: Solid state
    Reason: Low power/size/robust/ transfer rate

    Web Server
    Storage: Magnetic
    Reason: Large capacity/low cost per Mb

    DVD
    Storage: Optical
    Reason: Portable/read by range of devices

(f) Random Access Memory

18. (a) (i) Line 17

    (ii) Line 20

    (iii) Line 16

(b) *State:* Syntax

(c) (i) *State:* Conditional (loop)

    (ii) *State:* Real number >20 and <70

(d) *State:*
    Structure Chart
    Structure Diagram
    Flow Chart

(e) *State:* Interpreter

    Explain: No need to leave the programming environment/tracing facilities/debugging facilities

(f) Interface

19. (a) (i) 1 mark for showing a linear design
            1 mark for all arrows

    (ii) *Explain:* Carbon Footprint is the overall harmful emissions associated with a life of a product/time frame

(iii) *Explain:* Logic error executes but gives wrong answer

    Calculation incorrectly implemented

(b) (i) *Identify:*
    Selection: user clicks on tile
    Repetition: repeat turn/repeat tile turning until tiles matched/repeat game

    (ii) *Candidate should specify energy saving tip relating to image.*
    For example:

    Diagram 1:
    Switch off device when not in use to save energy.
    Don't leave devices on standby when not in use.

    Diagram 2:
    Laptops use less power.
    Switch laptop to hibernate when not in use.
    Reduce brightness to save power.
    Dispose of laptops correctly

    (iii) *Explain:*
    Demonstrate understanding of copying work created by others.
    For example:
    - Use of images without copyright permission
    - Plagiarism of other person's writing

    (iv) *State:*
    Faster transfer/download speed
    Downloading via mobile might use up data (allowance)

20. (a) *Code:*
    ```
    REPEAT 6
    move(n)
    rotate(60)
    END REPEAT
    ```

(b) *Describe any one from:*
    - Internal commentary
    - Meaningful identifiers
    - Modularisation
    - White space
    - Indentation

(c) *Any suitable function. Apply knowledge to the scenario.*
    For example:
    - Polygon (any shape)
    - Text tool
    - Fill

(d) 8
    45

(e) Square required complete attributes, eg:
    startx, starty
    length, rotation, line fill

(f) *State:*
    Structure Chart or
    Flow Diagram/Chart

21. (a) (i) *Identify:*

EXHIBITOR table	PRODUCT table
exhibitor code company name area stand number	exhibitor code product ref item name price

  (ii) *Identify:* Exhibitor code

(b) *Name:*
   Object
   Graphic
   Container

(c) *Name:* Presence check

(d) (i) *Identify from diagram:*
   • Large areas to make selection easy
   • Large readable text
   • Uncluttered screen

  (ii) • Macro/Script/search program activated
   • Search carried out using
     Area field = Tech Zone

(e) *Identify any two from:*
   • Breadcrumb
   • Highlighted selection
   • Back/Forward buttons
   • Search (bar)
   • Home (button)

NATIONAL 5 COMPUTING SCIENCE 2015

Section 1

1. 1 0 1 0 0 1 0 0

2. Integer

3 (age >= 5) AND (age <=18)
   2 conditions correct — 1 mark
   AND — 1 mark

4. Shortcuts/favourites/bookmarks/
   refresh/stop button/home button/search box/address
   bar/tabbed browsing

   Change user settings (font size etc.)
   Change default homepage
   Customising toolbars

5. Normal
      >=1 and <=80 (1 mark)
   Exceptional
      <1 or >80 (1 mark)
   Any example of text

6. Suitable reason why the links are inconsistent

7. The user will be required to enter a password (1 mark)
   Until the correct password is entered (1 mark)

8. *Any one valid:*
   • Upload/transfer faster
   • More files can be stored

9. *Any two of:*
   • Emphasise keywords
   • Internal commentary
   • Indentation
   • White space
   • Meaningful identifiers
   • Modular code
   • Use of parameter passing

10. String

11. Easier to backup files (1)
    Easier to implement different levels of access (security) (1)
    Centralised storage (1)
    Users have usernames and passwords (1)

12. Communications (Act)

13. Description of sensitive information (PIN, passwords etc)
    being logged.

14. *Any one valid answer for wired:*
    • It's more secure/security
    • It's more reliable/reliability
    • Upload/download speed faster

15. • Matches user interface (correct layout)
    • Spelling/Grammar
    • Graphic quality
    • Colour scheme useable
    • Graphics load correctly
    • Works on multiple browsers

Section 2

16. (a) *Any two suitable features relating to user interface:*
    • Interactive elements such as buttons all same
      shape, size, colour
    • Appropriate navigation
    • Consistent/appropriate layout of elements
    • Consistent colour theme
    • Accessibility Options

(b) The web page code/HTML/CSS determines the appearance of the web page not the browser

(c) (i) *Answer should name any standard file format for graphics:*
- gif
- bmp
- png

(ii) Relative

(iii) 4 × 6 × 600 × 600 (1 mark)
× 24 bits (1 mark)
(207360000 bits/8/1024/1024)
= 24.72 Mb (1 mark)

(d) *A description that includes:*
- Matching keywords/search criteria entered by user
- Database of known pages/stored metadata

17. (a) Mantissa and exponent

(b) (i) Interpreter

(ii) *Any one for 1 mark:*
- Additional RAM required
- Increased processing required
- (Could run more slowly)
- Loops translated multiple times

(c) Machine Code or Binary

(d) (i) Address Bus

(ii) Data Bus

(iii) Arithmetic Logic Unit (ALU)

(e) *Any two for 1 mark each:*
- Temporary storage of data
- Handling of status signals
- Data conversion – serial to parallel
- Voltage conversion
- Communication between two devices

18. (a) *Answer identifies one aim of school learner section of SQA site:*
- Provide information about exams
- Provide resources to help study for exams

(b) Domain name of URL:
(www.)sqa.org.uk

(c) (i) *Any one from the following:*
- Listen to the page option
- Text resize option
- Change colour scheme/Alter background colour
- Read transcript of video

(ii) • Screen reader reads out text of page and graphic captions to help those with sight problems or reading difficulty to access page content.
- Text resize option can be used by those with visual impairment to enlarge text making it easier to see and read.
- Changing colour scheme allows people with dyslexia or colour blindness or vision problems to access content.
- Altering colour combinations makes text easier to distinguish.
- Transcript of video makes video content accessible to those with hearing impairment.

(d) Gif

(e) • Helps user view path taken to reach this page
- Useful to retrace steps and go back to previous pages
- Useful in indicating section of current page to orientate user

(f)

2014 NQ Examination – Personal Timetable Builder

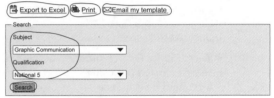

(g) *Complex sort described:*
- Date ascending
- Time ascending

(h) • Containing a virus
- May not have correct software
- File may be too large

19. (a) • Line 2 – Integer
- Line 3 – Real
- Line 5 – Boolean

(b) (i) • Line 6
- Line 9

(ii) Arithmetic Logic Unit (ALU)

(c) (i) An array (1 mark)
Of Reals (1 mark)

(ii) Unconditional/fixed loop (1 mark)
The program loops a known (12) number of times. (1 mark)

20. (a) Presence check
Length check/field length

(b) *Potential for increased errors due to:*
- Update anomalies
- Lots of changes being made

(c) (i) Unique identifier for a row/record in a table.

(ii) Dept ID
Product Code

(d) Boolean
Graphic/Object/Container

(e) *1 mark for each bullet (max 2):*
- Removing data from hard drive
- Using collection company
- Recycle individual components appropriately
- Dispose of dangerous elements

21. (a) *1 mark each for:*
- Conditional loop
- Input of brick length from user
- Correct complex conditions attached to loop (>15 AND <50)

(b) *1 mark each for:*
- Assignment
  any relevant example
- Calculating wall area
  lengthOfWall * heightOfWall
- Calculating brick area
  lengthOfBrick * heightOfBrick
- Dividing wall area by brick area

(c) A function could be used to remove the decimal places from the number (1 mark) and then 1 could be added on (1 mark).
or
int(numberOFBricks) + 1

Marks allocated as:
int(numberOFBricks) (1 mark)
+ 1 (1 mark)

(d) 4

22. (a) *Any two from:*
- Solid state has no moving parts
- Camera is portable, size/weight of storage should be considered
- Robust storage more suitable
- Solid state can be removed
- Transfer/storage of data faster to/from solid state

(b) Total storage (1 mark)
64Gb = 64 × 1024 = 65,536 (Mb)

Number of photos (1 mark)
65,536/25 = 2,621.44
rounded down to 2621 photos

(c) *Any two advantages of tablet PC over laptop relevant to scenario:*
- Simple interface for range of users/guests
- Touch screen easy to use for guests
- More portability to pass round at event/lightweight
- More robust when being passed around

(d) (i) *Use of cloud:*
- Remote access from any location with internet connection
- Centrally accessible storage location
- Provide login to guests who can access the files on their own device

(ii) Cross-platform OS compatibility — runs on variety of operating systems

(e) *Concerns about Wifi:*
- Slow data transfer speed compared to wired connection
- Security issues
- Limited range/lack of coverage/loss of connection in parts of venue
- Signal interference from other devices

NATIONAL 5 COMPUTING SCIENCE 2016

1. 1 1 1 0 0 0 1 1

2. Easier to edit/maintain.
   or
   Another programmer can understand the code.

3. The database cannot be edited.

4. *Any one from:*
- No typing error/human error
- Only one can be selected
- Limits possible inputs
- Appropriate input when no keyboard, for example touchscreen device

5. To store data temporarily.

6. *Any two from:*
- Firewall
- Spam killer
- Spyware protection
- Malware protection (Trojan)
- Biometric (software)
- Email protection
- Parental control
- Privacy
- Phishing protection
- Encryption (software)
- Password manager
- Backup
- Social network protection

7.
- Phishing
- Malware\spyware
- Hacking
- Virus
- Trojan

8. Expert

9. *All three bullets for 2 marks:*
- Program loops/program repeats lines 3 and 4/program checks condition
- A message is displayed
- Another temperature reading is taken
Any two bullets for 1 mark.
One or **zero** bullets: no marks.

10. Search **or** Query

11. 1. Compiler (1)
    2. Interpreter (1)

12. *1 mark each for:*
- Loop 16 times
- Input of time from user inside loop

13. *Description of two problems and improvements from poor navigation list below:*
- Navigation in two different places
- Navigation not labelled correctly (buttons along top, 'radio buttons', 'check boxes', 'new' button, 'arrow' button)
- No indication of which page (1,2,3,4,5) the user is currently on
- No indication where login will take you
One mark for each problem and improvement required.
If candidate states two problems without improvements award **one** mark.

14. Peer to Peer **or** P2P

15. (a) *Any one from:*
    - Route ID data value is not unique
    - Cannot identify one row in the table using Route ID data value

    (b) *Any two problems from:*
    - Data duplication
    - Inconsistency of data
    - Update anomalies

    (c) Relational (database)
    or
    Linked (tables)

    (d) Text

    (e) (i) *Any one from:*
    - Restricted (choice)
    - Presence check

    (ii) Exceptional (1 mark):
    - Any value less than 1 or
    - Any value greater than 6 or
    - And real value
    - Any example of text value

    Extreme (1 mark):
    - 1
    or
    - 6

    (f) *Two fields in correct order with sorting direction:*
    - Price ascending
    - Depart ascending

16. (a) *Design or code should include the following bullet points for 1 mark each:*
    - Loop
    - Loop condition
    - User input, numTwo re-entered after condition (or within loop...until)
    - Error message to user

    (b) Character (char)

    (c) Output would be:
    "Correct it is in the middle"

    (d) *1 mark for each:*
    - Random (Number)
    - To generate a random value between two values
    or
    - Between a range
    or
    - Between limits

    (e) Lines 3 to 17 (or 3 to 18) should be placed inside a loop (1 mark)
    Repeat 10 times (1 mark)

17. (a) Hierarchical

    (b) *Description or naming of:*
    - Storyboard
    - Wireframe

    (c) *Description of function of hyperlink:*
    - Provides navigation through a website
    - Click on hyperlink to move to another resource (page)

    (d) (i) Video
    (ii) Looking for path and filename
    resources/dunk.gif

    (e) (i) (Hyper)link to another website
    (ii) Uniform Resource Locator

    (iii) Calculating Resolution (1 mark) 7x600x5x600
    Multiplying by Colour depth (1 mark)
    (12600000x24)
    Convert to Megabytes (1 mark)
    /8/1024/1024 = 36.048 Megabytes

18. (a) (i) Increase file size
    (ii) mp3
    Alternative compressed audio formats are acceptable (but not mp4 as this is a container file for storing video)

    (b) (i) Hacking
    or
    Unauthorised access
    (ii) *Description of one other offence under CMA:*
    - Unauthorised access with intent to commit crime/further offences
    - Unauthorised modification of data

    (c) Communications Act

    (d) (i) Graphics are owned by someone else
    or
    Without permission he would break the Copyright, Designs & patents Act

    (ii) *Selection construct with appropriate condition (1 mark):*
    - IF answer = A
    - IF answer = correct answer
    - IF question 3 = A
    Assignment to update totalscore variable (1 mark):
    - totalscore TO totalscore + 1
    - add one to score
    - totalscore = + 1

    (e) *Any two for 1 mark each:*
    - Right to view own personal data
    - Right to have own data corrected if incorrect
    - Right to seek compensation for damages caused by inaccurate information
    - Right to prevent data being used for direct marketing
    - Right to ask for data to be deleted (if it breaches the DPA principles)

19. (a) Array (1 mark)
    Of Real (1 mark)

    (b) (i) *Description includes reference to:*
    - Line 1 – total set to 0
    - Line 3 – loop
    - Line 4 – each cost is added to previous total

    (ii) Mantissa (1 mark)
    Exponent (1 mark)

    (iii) Error in question code
    A
    Accept any answer that would have explained the total being incorrect:
    - Logic error
    - Syntax error (DUE)
    - Not recompiled code
    - Program not saved before being re-run
    - Program only calculates 5 costs
    - Program has not been run
    - Has not added on the 45.00
    - Line 3 has not been implemented correctly
    B
    1 mark for stating how error could be corrected

(c) Used to join text and variables together
or
Output includes both text and variables together
or
Used to join strings

20. (a) Blocks attempts to access a device
or
Filters incoming traffic

(b) Encryption encodes a file (1) so that it is unreadable (1) by others

(c) (i) *Any Input device from:*
- Touch screen
- Digital camera
- Microphone

Any Output device from:
- (HD) display
- Speakers

(ii) *Any Interface type device from:*
- USB (3)
- (Micro) HDMI
- Headphone jack

(iii) *Any one for 1 mark from:*
- Temporary storage of data
- Handling of status signals
- Data conversion – serial to parallel
- Voltage conversion
- Communication between devices

(iv) *Two reasons for incompatibility (1 mark each):*
- OS version too old (4.1 needs 4.4 or higher)
- Lack of storage(16 Gigabyte needs 32 Gigabyte)

(d) *One reason that describes difference in interaction between user and device:*
- Smartphone screen size much smaller so less room for text and menus to be displayed
- Input device used to make selection is touch screen so need larger icons and text than can be selected using touch input
- smartphone interface has fewer objects allowing for faster download to portable device

21. (a) (i) *Any one from:*
- Provides a visual representation which can be easier to understand
- Illustrates flow of data/sequence of processes

(ii) Input validation

(b) IF/while (1 mark)
numPlayers <=4 (1 mark)
numGames <=3 (1 mark)
or
numPlayers <5 (1 mark)
numGames <4 (1 mark)

(c) (i)

Test data type	Expected result
Normal	Booking accepted
Extreme	Booking accepted
Exceptional	**Not valid number of players**

(ii) Run time/Execution error

(d) *Any one from:*
- Internal commentary
- Meaningful identifiers
- Indentation/white space
- Highlight keywords
- Modular code

Acknowledgements

Permission has been sought from all relevant copyright holders and Hodder Gibson is grateful for the use of the following:

Image © slava296/Shutterstock.com (2014 page 8);
Image © Perfect Vectors/Shutterstock.com (2014 page 8);
Image © A-R-T/Shutterstock.com (2014 page 22);
Image © Kostsov/Shutterstock.com (2014 page 22);
Image © wwwebmeister/Shutterstock.com (2014 page 22);
Image © Nicholas 852/Shutterstock.com (2014 page 22);
Image © Pavel Ignatov/Shutterstock.com (2014 page 22);
Image © Duna Csongor/Shutterstock.com (2014 page 22);
Image © Pavel Ignatov/Shutterstock.com (2014 page 23);
Image © wwwebmeister/Shutterstock.com (2014 page 23);
Image © A-R-T/Shutterstock.com (2014 page 23);
Image © Hubis/Shutterstock.com (2015 page 8);
Image © Rashevskyi Viacheslav/Shutterstock.com (2015 page 21);
Image © Matthew Cole/Shutterstock.com (2015 page 21);
Image © musicman/Shutterstock.com (2015 page 28);
Image © JMiks/Shutterstock.com (2016 page 4);
Image © Tatiana Popova/Shutterstock.com (2016 page 5);
Image © Linusy/Shutterstock.com (2016 page 7);
Image © Neirfy/Shutterstock.com (2016 pages 18 & 19).